Urban Flooding & Rainwater Harvesting

Urban Flooding & Rainwater Harvesting

Urban Flooding and Rainwater Harvesting
With Specific Reference to India

Hema Kanta Barua

EXCELLER BOOKS®
A GLOBAL PRESS

Urban Flooding and Rainwater Harvesting

Cover by Exceller Books using resources from Pixabay.com

ISBN: 978-93-48892-56-0

First published in India in 2025 by Exceller Books,
An imprint of GE Group

Address: G1, Dream Apartment, Degree College Road, Belgharia,
Kolkata, 700056, India
www.excellerbooks.com

EXCELLER BOOKS®
A GLOBAL PRESS

DEDICATED TO

My mother
Late Purneswari Barua

My father
Late Tankeswar Barua

Acknowledgement

I take great pride in expressing my heartfelt thanks to Prof. (Dr.) Dristi Neog, a distinguished Professor of a reputed university in the USA, for writing the Foreword of this book. She is also my brilliant and beloved niece. As an ardent admirer of her academic achievements, I felt it was only natural to invite her to contribute, and she graciously agreed. A gifted scholar, she earned B. Arch. From SPA, JNTU Hyderabad and went on to complete her Master's (in city and regional planning) from the University of Texas at Arlington, Texas, and Ph. D. (urban and regional planning) from Florida State University, Florida, in the United States. She authored the book *Shaping the Future: Community Planning Basics for Healthier, Happier and More Sustainable Cities.* In addition, she has published widely in peer-reviewed journals. We are proud of her, and I extend my blessings for her continued success.

A discussion was held with the experienced engineers of the Engineers' Club of Jorhat (Assam) on a particular evening of the last year. It was that discussion that motivated me strongly to write this book with the primary objective of creating effective awareness about different aspects of urban flooding and rainwater harvesting among urban citizens in general, and among engineers associated with the urbanization process in particular. I am deeply grateful to the members of this Engineers' Club.

I have consulted a wide range of books, publications, and guidelines from various institutions, organisations, and individuals in writing this book. The most notable ones are listed in the Reference Section. I express my thanks and gratitude to all of them.

At the end, I would like to thank the team members of Excellar Books for their significant contribution in bringing the book to market on time and to the desired quality.

Contents

Foreword

Over the years, I've closely followed Dr. Hema Kanta Barua's work and have long admired his ability to bring engineering solutions to life. His work is always grounded in local context and informed by decades of practical experience. *Urban Flooding and Rainwater Harvesting* is a natural extension of that legacy: a timely, essential contribution to one of the most pressing urban challenges today.

As a professor of sustainability and urban planning at Westfield State University in Massachusetts, USA, my career has focused on building healthier, more livable, and more resilient cities. Through research, teaching, and writing, including my book *Shaping Our Future: Community Planning Basics for Happier, Healthier, and More Sustainable Cities,* I've explored how planning, infrastructure, and public awareness intersect to drive long-term sustainability. So when Dr. Barua invited me to write this foreword, the connection felt immediate. This book brings together everything I care about: practical solutions, sustainability, and a clear vision for how cities can do better. I find this book deeply aligned with my own work. This book speaks directly to that mission, taking up the pressing urban issue of flooding and the underutilized potential of rainwater harvesting in Indian cities, especially in the Northeast Region of India.

It addresses a critical and recurring crisis, urban flooding, which continues to disrupt infrastructure, health, mobility, and daily life in cities across India—including Guwahati, in Assam, located in the Northeast Region of the country. Dr. Barua draws on a rich career spanning teaching, research, structural engineering, policy engagement, and fieldwork to offer both a clear diagnosis of the problem and a comprehensive, practical path forward.

What I love most about this book is how it goes beyond just talking about problems. It explains in clear, accessible language what causes urban flooding and then lays out real, doable strategies to manage it, especially through rainwater harvesting. It's written not just for technical experts, but for city leaders, educators, infrastructure users, and concerned citizens alike. From identifying root causes to outlining implementable drainage and rainwater harvesting solutions, this book is both a practical guide and a source of hope. Readers will discover that the book offers them both a clear understanding of the problem and a comprehensive set of practical, implementable solutions.

As climate change intensifies old challenges and cities increasingly seek scalable solutions, this book stands out. It is informative, approachable, and, most importantly, actionable. I encourage readers across disciplines to engage with its insights and apply its recommendations. Dr. Barua reminds us that many solutions are already within reach and shows us how we can move forward with confidence.

Dr. Dristi Neog

Professor, Department of Geography, Planning, and Sustainability

Westfield State University

Preface

Objective

The issue of urban flooding and rainwater harvesting has become a globally recognized concern today. During the last few decades, the technologies, techniques, policies, guidelines and materials have developed substantially in respect of addressing this issue. Against this scenario of availability of technology, techniques and guidelines, it has been strongly felt by the author during his long professional life in teaching, research and construction over a period of more than half a century that there does exist a tremendous gap between the available knowledge and its application on the ground of cities/towns. The reason for the different problems created by the intensifying issue of urban flooding in many Indian cities/towns may be attributed primarily to this factor *(i.e., the gap between available knowledge and its utilization on the ground).* The realization of the extent of this gap has been the main force motivating the author to write this book. The primary objective of writing this small book has been to contribute to the aspect of creating awareness among all those involved in the process of urbanization. The book makes an attempt to deal with some of the salient aspects bearing on this issue through a set of three chapters, each having only a few pages.

Targeted Readers

All the stakeholders of the process of urbanization, including the technicians, budding engineers, practicing engineers in different roles, contractors, owners and users of different infrastructure, teachers of technical institutes etc. are expected to derive benefits from the different contents of the book, as briefly reflected in the *Organizations and Brief Contents of Chapters (given below).*

Organizations and Brief Contents of Chapters

Each chapter starts with an *Introduction* and ends with a *Concluding Remark.* The different topics dealt with in the book have been organized in the following order.

Chapter I deals with, in general, the different aspects of *'Urban Flooding and its Management in India with Reference to NER'*.

The different techniques of rainwater harvesting have been briefly discussed in Chapter II under the broad heading of *'Different Techniques of Rainwater Harvesting in Urban Areas'*.

Chapter III deals with the basic objective of writing this book - the different aspects of *'Public Awareness — a Salient Aspect of the Management of Urban Drainage System'*.

A large body of available literature on the relevant areas has been consulted in writing this book. The salient ones are listed under *References,* which appear at the end of the book.

Hema Kanta Barua
Guwahati, Assam
April, 2025

Chapter 1

Urban Flooding and Its Management in India With Reference to NER

1.1. Introduction

As stated in the guidelines of UN[1], the number of people affected by natural disasters in the world was 147 million (on average) per year during the period from 1981 to 1990. It increased to 211 million per year during the period from 1991 to 2000. Furthermore, it was noted[1] that flooding alone accounted for over two-thirds of those affected, thereby indicating the significant global impact caused by flooding. However, this discussion is limited only to *urban flooding* (not to the general flood, i.e. *the natural flooding (riverine) covering large extents of rural areas).*

Urban flooding has become a well-known phenomenon worldwide. Numerous studies have been conducted on the causes of urban flooding and its management. In India, too, waterlogging and flooding across different cities/towns have been causing complex situations, resulting in manifold sufferings for citizens, apart from economic losses on various fronts. At the outset, it is essential to understand the broad types of urban flooding. As stated in the report[4], the broad types of urban flooding are pluvial, riverine (fluvial) and coastal. A city or a town, depending on its location, may experience only pluvial flooding or a combination of pluvial flooding with riverine or coastal flooding. The discussion in this article has been limited to urban flooding of the pluvial type, as most cities and towns in India experience this type of flooding today. An attempt has been made in this article to discuss this issue in the Indian context with reference to the cities/towns of NER under the broad subheads of:

- Reasons for urban flooding,
- Basic approach to the adoption of remedial measures,
- Planning and designing of drainage systems in cities/towns,
- Maintenance of drainage systems and
- Concluding remarks

The primary objective of this discussion has been to raise awareness among all stakeholders in India about the technological advancements in managing urban flooding of the pluvial type.

1.2. Reasons of Urban Flooding

The basic reason for urban flooding is summarily the haphazard urbanization in India, coupled with the lack of awareness *(among the stakeholders of urban development, including the citizens of cities/towns)* about the available policies and guidelines[2,3,4] well set by the Ministry of Housing and Urban Development, researchers and others. While examining the various reasons leading to urban flooding, three broad categories of existing drainage systems in India's cities and towns have emerged. These categories are:

- Cities/towns having no scientifically planned, designed, executed and properly maintained drainage system,
- Cities/towns having a well-maintained drainage system, but not properly planned and designed, and executed with inadequate data, including rainfall data, and
- Cities/towns having a drainage system, properly planned, designed, and executed with adequate data, but not properly maintained.

Most of the cities/towns in India fall under the first category. In cities falling under this category, the process of urbanization has been growing rapidly in the absence of a duly prepared Master Plan, of which a proper Drainage

System Plan is a key component. The developmental activities associated with growing urbanization, in the absence of a technically prepared Master Plan *(which needs to be reviewed periodically)*, lead to a series of issues that contribute to urban flooding. The storm runoff in cities/towns has been increasing due to several factors. The salient ones have been briefly dealt with below.

1.2.1. Increase in Intensity of Rainfall

Global climate change has been primarily responsible for causing an appreciable increase in both the frequency and intensity of precipitation (rainfall). For a useful discussion, the rainfall data for Guwahati city of Assam, as given by Weather Underground[6], appearing in table 1.1, have been critically looked into in view of the fact that the urban flooding (in this city) has been intensifying. A critical analysis of the situation in this city enables one to appreciate the reasons for urban flooding in India.

Months \ Year	Precipitation in inches in 2019			Precipitation in inches in 2020			Precipitation in inches in 2021		
	Max*	Av.**	Total***	Max*	Av**	Total***	Max*	Av**	Total***
February	0.00	0.00	0.00	0.31	0.02	0.47	0.28	0.01	0.28
March	0.00	0.00	0.00	0.47	0.03	0.97	1.69	0.07	2.06
April	0.04	0.00	0.06	1.97	0.30	9.11	1.81	0.17	5.14
May	0.00	0.00	0.00	2.68	0.46	14.15	0.87	0.21	6.53
June	0.00	0.00	0.00	1.77	0.46	13.92	2.24	0.35	10.48
July	0.00	0.00	0.00	0.98	0.25	7.68	1.93	0.24	7.34
August	0.28	0.01	0.32	3.78	0.22	6.74	0.87	0.11	3.33
September	2.72	0.40	12.14	2.36	0.34	10.07	4.76	0.25	7.53
October	3.62	0.19	5.91	2.05	0.07	2.18	1.34	0.07	2.20
Novemer	0.51	0.02	0.62	0.00	0.00	0.00	0.00	0.00	0.00

(a) For years 2019, 2020 & 2021

Months \ Year	Precipitation in inches in 2022			Precipitation in inches in 2023			Precipitation in inches in 2024		
	Max*	Av.**	Total***	Max*	Av**	Total***	Max*	Av**	Total***
February	0.79	0.07	1.86	0.00	0.00	0.00	0.12	0.01	0.20
March	0.16	0.01	0.20	1.97	0.24	7.40	1.10	0.06	2.01
April	0.87	0.16	4.88	1.14	0.14	4.30	2.36	0.10	2.89
May	2.05	0.37	11.49	1.02	0.19	5.85	1.73	0.31	9.52
June	3.11	0.66	19.71	1.81	0.45	13.44	2.76	0.48	14.37
July	2.36	0.22	6.81	2.13	0.22	6.73	2.48	0.31	9.47
August	2.95	0.20	6.06	0.63	0.11	3.47	1.97	0.34	10.39
September	1.38	0.11	3.23	1.30	0.13	3.92	1.10	0.11	3.29
October	2.28	0.20	6.27	1.38	0.14	4.39	1.30****	0.21	5.31
Novemer	0.00	0.00	0.00	0.00	0.00	0.00	----	-----	-----

Maximum precipitation on a day in the month, **Average daily precipitation in the month, ***Total precipitation in the month, ** Record only up to 25th of October 2024*

(b) For years 2022, 2023 & 2024

Table 1.1: Precipitation Data for Guwahati (Assam) City of India for Last Six Years (2019 – 2024) (Prepared by the author on the basis of the data of Weather Undergroun[6])

Figure 1.1 has been further developed for:

- Variation of maximum rainfall on a day year-wise and
- Variation of total rainfall year-wise for six years (from February to November, as included in table 1.1) for the city of Guwahati.

The analysis of table 1.1 and figure 1.1 reveals several key observations regarding urban flooding, as outlined below.

- *Observation 1:* The highest precipitation *(rainfall, not storm water)* in a day in the month of September in 2021 (Table 1.1 & Figure 1.1a). This is equivalent to approximately 121 mm, which is comparable to 108 mm, the highest rainfall in a single day recorded in Delhi in 2024. However, as evidenced by figure 1.1a, the maximum precipitation in a single day over the last three years (2022, 2023, and 2024) has been lower than that for 2021.

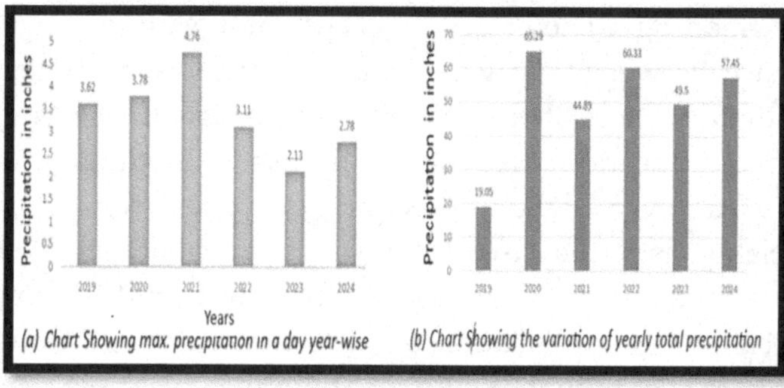

(a) Chart Showing max. precipitation in a day year-wise *(b) Chart Showing the variation of yearly total precipitation*

Figure 1.1: Charts Showing Variation of (A) Max. Precipitation in A Day Year-Wise & (B) Yearly Total Precipitation for Guwahati City (Prepared by the Author on the Basis of Data Appearing in table 1).

- *Observation 2*: The highest total precipitation of 65.29 inches (1658 mm) in a year occurred in 2020 *(Figure 1.1 b)*. In this case, too, there has been a trend of reduction in total precipitation in the last four years (2021, 2022, 2023, and 2024), as evidenced by figure 1.1b. The average annual precipitation for the six-year period (2019-2024, as shown in figure 1.1b) is 49.42 inches (1255 mm). This annual average rainfall is appreciably low compared to that for the whole state of Assam, which is 2818 mm, as per Rainwater Harvesting Data[8].

- *Observation 3:* The data in table 1.1 and figure 1.1 do not suggest an aggravation of the rainfall situation in the city of Guwahati, particularly over the last four years. In fact, there appears to be a stable (if not slightly decreasing) trend of rainfall. In view of this trend of rainfall in Guwahati city, the necessity of examining the reasons responsible for aggravating the situation of urban flooding has assumed a greater dimension today.

It is not solely the rainfall (precipitation) that leads to urban flooding. It is truly the stormwater that causes the urban flooding. Therefore, a clear understanding of the difference between rainwater and stormwater facilitates the basic identification of the factors causing urban flooding. At this stage, a question arises as to why urban flooding becomes aggravated even when precipitation does not increase appreciably, as in the case of the city of Guwahati, as reflected in the above-noted three observations. It is indeed in this context that the appreciation of the basic reasons responsible for creating aggravating urban flooding in most Indian cities/towns today requires the identification of the factors causing the difference in the volumes of rain and stormwater. As normally expected, the volume of storm water flowing over the earth's surface (in urban areas) should be less than that of the rainwater. However, in the case of most cities and towns experiencing urban flooding, this is not the case. To understand the phenomenon of urban flooding, it is essential to comprehend urban hydrology, particularly in relation to the hydrological cycle, which has been thoroughly examined in the IWP Report[4]. A schematic diagram summarizing the salient features of the hydrological cycle, which involves the continuous transport of water masses from the sea and back to the sea, has been developed in its simplest form based on input from this report[4], as shown in figure 1.2.

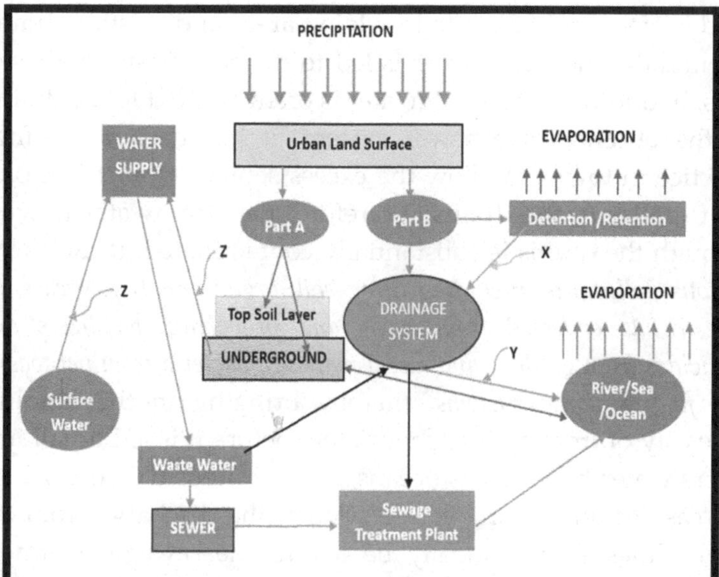

Part A & Part B constitute the total rainfall on the land surface (discussed in the text), X-----Water is led to the Detention Pond (not from Retention Water Body) Y----- Very often storm water is led to river/sea, Z------- Water supply either from the surface or from the underground

Figure 1.2: Hydrological Cycle of Rainwater on Urban Land Surface (Prepared by the Author on the Basis of the Input Derived From IWP Report[4]).

The precipitation (or the rainfall) occurs on account of the evaporation of water primarily from the sea/ocean (though to a lesser extent from the water of other sources such as rivers/water bodies, including retention lakes). It falls on the urban land surface, splitting into two parts — Part A and Part B, as indicated in figure 1.2. Part A comprises different portions of rainwater, namely a portion absorbed as evaporation of rainwater from the land surface, a portion absorbed by the roots of plants existing on the land surface and the third part being the portion absorbed by the top surface of land in its onward movement into the underground in the natural process. Part B constitutes the portion of the rainwater flowing over the land surface following the gradient. This is the storm runoff that carries debris from the land surface and falls into low-lying areas and existing drains. Eventually, the stormwater is led to the river/water bodies/or seas. In addition, the wastewater is often also led to the drains. In the absence of a sewer system, it has been a common practice in towns to allow the excess septage from the choke-pit to fall into the drains. Therefore, the stormwater flowing through the drains is substantially contaminated. It can carry[4] *various pollutants, including litter, soil, organic matter, grease, oil and metals collected from roads and properties; fertilizers and pesticides from gardens and faecal material; bacteria from pet wastes and failing septic systems,* thereby bringing in the absolute necessity of treating it appropriately before it is led to fall into rivers/water bodies/seas/oceans, as indicated in figure 1.2. In the case of an existing sewer system, the discharge from the sewer lines should ideally be led to the sewage treatment plant, as shown in figure 1.2. The treated water may be led to the river/sea/ocean, as is the normal practice. However, a portion of this (if not wholly) may be reused for purposes other than drinking. As seen, in most of the cities/towns, the sewage treatment plant does not exist (or inadequately exists), and the storm water from drains is directly led to the river/sea/ocean/water bodies (as indicated by 'Y' in the figure). Figure 1.2, therefore, briefly represents the complete hydrological cycle of rainwater starting from 'river-sea-ocean' and back to 'river-sea-ocean', as it has been briefly discussed.

The 'reasons for urban flooding' and 'remedial measures for urban flooding' truly emerge from a deep analysis of the hydrological cycle of rainwater, as described through figure 1.2. The process of urbanization significantly alters the hydrological cycle of rainwater in cities/towns. This change primarily results from the increase in imperviousness of soil in urban areas, changes in land use, and an increase in catchment area (depending on location), among other factors. These factors are briefly discussed below.

1.2.2. Increase in the Imperviousness of Soil in Urban Area

The imperviousness continues to increase with the process of urbanization due to the creation of impervious surfaces, such as asphalt and concrete roads, concrete sidewalls, roofs, and parking places.

- *Change in Land Use:* Forest and agricultural lands are being converted for various urban development activities in most cities and towns in India. Many low-lying areas and natural water bodies are being converted for housing and other developmental activities as part of the urbanization process.
- *Increase in Catchment Area:* This factor becomes predominant in most cities and towns surrounded, either partly or fully, by hills. The devastation of forests and the cutting of hills for various developmental activities results in the flow of stormwater into urban areas located at or near the base of the hills. A clear example of Guwahati City of Assam may be cited. The case of this city is discussed in greater detail later in this article.

1.2.3. Encroachment on Banks of Natural/Man-Made Channels/Drains

The encroachment on banks of channels/drains has been a common practice in many cities and towns in our country for various purposes, thereby reducing the cross-sectional areas.

The change in the hydrological cycle of rainfall in cities and towns, due to the primary factors briefly discussed above, is indeed the basic reason leading to the situation of urban flooding. The increase in the volume of storm runoff causes the overflow of existing drains, thereby causing the urban flood.

1.3. Basic Approach to the Adoption of Remedial Measures

The increase in the volume of storm runoff, as discussed under subhead 1.2, is basically the reason for urban flooding in most of the cities/towns in India. The situation of urban flooding has been exacerbated by additional secondary factors, such as the reduction in the carrying capacity of the existing drainage system. This reduction is caused by a number of factors, as briefly stated earlier. An approach to tackling the issue of urban flooding fundamentally consists of adopting different measures, as suggested by various studies. The general approach basically includes an attempt:

- To reduce the volume of storm runoff and/or
- To maintain the original design capacity of the drainage system in case of a properly designed drainage system.

These two broad aspects are briefly described below.

The various measures necessary for reduction emerge from the reasons leading to changes in the hydrological cycle of rainwater, as discussed with reference to figure 1.2 (subhead 1.2). The increase in imperviousness brings in the necessity of rainwater harvesting at both the individual and ULB levels. Secondly, the creation of detention and/or retention lakes should be taken into consideration with due regard to topographical situations and suitable locations. Thirdly, if necessary, the carrying capacity of the existing drainage system will be enhanced based on the necessary technical data. Finally, the maintenance of the drainage systems needs to be taken up on the basis of the policy guidelines[4,5]. These salient points are dealt with in greater detail below with reference to the intensifying urban flooding of Guwahati City.

The map showing the existing land use (as of 2021) of the Guwahati Metropolitan Area, taken from the Connective Cities[9], is given in figure 1.3. The total area of 328 Sq Km consists of two parts:

- Developed land of 144.87 Sq Km (44.2%) and
- Undeveloped land of 183.13 Sq Km (55.8%).

The break-up of these two parts is shown in table 1.2. As evident, the extent of undeveloped land (183.13 Sq Km) is substantially more than the developed land (144.87 Sq Km). This situation for the Guwahati City apparently suggests a series of measures which can be suitably adopted in light of *'the basic approach to the adoption of remedial measures'* (briefly dealt with above). In fact, it is appreciable to note that many measures are being taken by GMDA[9] in pursuit of the internationally accepted concept of sponge cities. The salient works[10] (planned or already executed) include:

- Implementation of Water Body (Preservation and Conservation) Act 2008 and development of water bodies,
- Construction of alternate stormwater drains at some basins,
- Installation of Automatic Weather Stations (AWS),
- Installation of Auto-priming MF pumps, etc.

In addition, other RCC drainage works (planned/executed) under the Mission Flood-Free Assam include the construction and extension of basin drains, the raising of guard walls along both sides of the Bharalu River, the construction of a concrete silt trap at the river Bharalu, and the construction of stormwater drains at various locations.

Developed land (Total = 144.87 Sq Km)			*Undeveloped land (Total = 183.13 Sq Km)*		
Land-use type	*Area (in Sq Km)*	*% of total**	*Land-use type*	*Area (in Sq Km)*	*% of total**
Residential	86.40	26.34	Vacant	43.70	13.32
Commercial	6.40	1.95	Agricultural	42.20	12.87
Industrial	5.75	1.75	Forest/Tree Clad	57.70	17.59
Mixed	2.72	0.83	Barren land	7.74	2.36
Public & Semipublic	22.98	7.01	Eco-friendly	5.80	1.77
Public Utilities	0.76	0.23	Waterbody	16.46	5.02
Recreational	2.72	0.83	Wetlands	8.00	2.44
Transportation	17.64	5.38	Aquaculture	1.53	0.47

*Percentages are based on total area of 328 Sg Km

Table 1.2: Break up the Existing Guwahati Metropolitan Area (Prepared by the Author on the Basis of Data Given by GMDA[9])

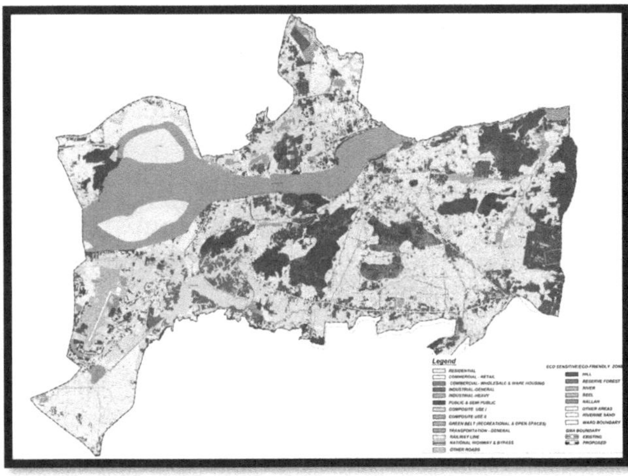

Figure 1.3: Map Showing the Land Use of Guwahati Metropolitan Area (Map Taken From Gmda[9])

The measures (planned/executed), as noted above, are obviously on the right track to mitigate the urban flooding of the city of Guwahati. However, in view of the intensifying situation, as recently observed, a question arises as to the adequacy and effectiveness of the same, particularly when the reasons (as discussed earlier in this Chapter) leading to the substantial increase in the volume of stormwater runoff causing the overflow of the existing drainage system are judiciously accounted for. It is in this context that aspects such as proper grading and the capacity of the existing drainage system, rainwater harvesting, and the creation of detention and retention ponds/lakes at appropriate locations come to the fore. Some of these aspects are discussed in greater detail below.

1.4. Rainwater Harvesting

The adoption of rainwater harvesting in urban areas becomes absolutely necessary for achieving the primary objectives of managing stormwater runoff, recharging groundwater, and ensuring sustainable water management practices. This aspect seems to be ignored in most of the growing urban areas, including cities like Guwahati. There is an abundance of available stock of knowledge and techniques today covering the different aspects of types and methods of rainwater harvesting. What is missing today in India is the lack of strict enforcement of appropriate bye-laws for the adoption of the technique. However, there do exist a number of standards, such as the ones[11,12,13] given under reference. As stated in the CPWD Manual[11], the Model Building Bye-laws, 2016, of the Ministry of Urban Development, has amply covered the provision for Rainwater Harvesting. As per these model bye-laws, *water harvesting through the storage of water runoff, including rainwater, in all building plots of 100 sqm and above, will be mandatory*. However, this provision does not appear to be duly honoured by many of the ULBs in the country. Nevertheless, there do exist provisions for rainwater conservation, rainwater recharging, and rainwater harvesting in most of the bye-laws of the country's states and UTs. For example, in the state of Assam, this provision is there in Appendix VI of *the Assam Unified Building Construction*

(Regulation) Bye-laws, 2022[14]. The responsibility of enforcing the said provisions lies with the ULBs of cities/towns. This is, indeed, an area warranting appropriate attention of all the stakeholders of urban areas suffering on account of the issue of urban flooding. In fact, the NDM Guidelines[3] have duly noted that every building in the urban area must have the provision of rainwater harvesting. The strict enforcement of this provision will lead to a substantial reduction in the volume of storm runoff.

1.5. Creation of Detention and Retention Ponds/Lakes

As already stated earlier, the impact of urbanization has been basically responsible for the issues leading to urban flooding. Therefore, the measures for mitigating this impact, including adequate facilities for detention and retention of storm runoff, need to be appropriately and adequately placed in position, as duly stressed by the NDM Guidelines[3]. This aspect appears to be ignored by most of the ULBs of cities/towns. The detention ponds are typically used for temporarily storing stormwater, particularly at locations with lower elevations, which can cause issues with providing the required gradient for the drainage system to achieve the appropriate gravity flow of stormwater through drains. Obviously, an appropriately designed pumping system must be placed in position to pump the stored water into the next part of the drainage system, provided at the required elevation. On the other hand, the retention tanks/lakes are water bodies for permanently storing storm water with the basic objective of reducing the volume of storm runoff through the drainage system, thereby reducing the possibilities of the overflowing of the storm water drains. Normally, some water bodies (ponds/lakes/wetlands) do exist in almost all cities/towns. However, the process of urbanization has been responsible for the extinction of many of these water bodies. Even for the existing ones, there has been a substantial reduction in their retaining capacity, basically due to encroachment on the boundaries on one hand and, on the other, due to heavy siltation for obvious reasons. The city of Guwahati has several wetlands (beels) that are affected by the adverse impacts of urbanization. However, some developmental activities[9] of these wetlands of Guwahati city are now being implemented. Most of the cities/towns facing the issue of urban flooding during the monsoon period are subjected to water scarcity in the dry season on account of the depleting groundwater table. It has been a genuine problem in the city of Guwahati, as most of its citizens are still dependent on underground water. Therefore, the adoption of the appropriate technique for recharging the groundwater aquifer has been an absolute necessity. Even in cases of detention/retention ponds/lakes, the provision of suitable measures for recharging the groundwater aquifer appears to be feasible and necessary as well. The second important aspect to be duly taken care of, prior to the outflow of stormwater into detention/retention ponds/lakes, is its treatment for the removal of pollutants. In addition to rejuvenating the existing water bodies in Guwahati city, the creation of more retention/detention tanks, particularly along the foothills within and around the boundaries of the master plan area, is recommended. Many developmental activities have been taking place in these hilly areas, resulting in issues with stormwater carrying large debris into the existing drainage system. This stormwater is responsible for creating heavy siltation in the existing water bodies and drains, adversely affecting their retention/carrying capacities.

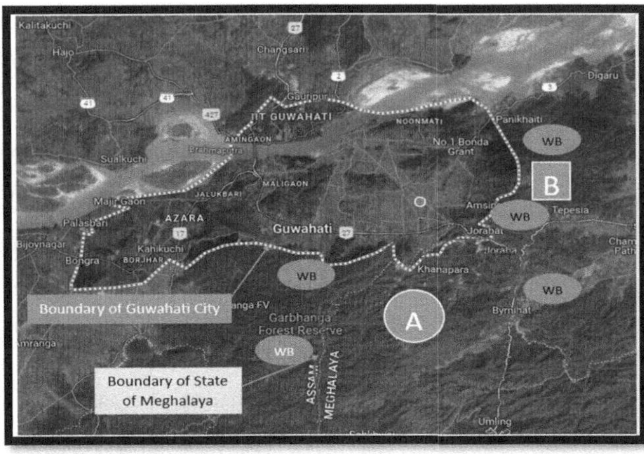

Figure 1.4: Google Map Showing the Catchment Area (Mkd. A & B) Outside the Boundary of Guwahati City

A significant amount of stormwater apparently enters the city's drainage system from the areas (Figure 1.4) marked as A (located in the state of Meghalaya) and B (located in the state of Assam).

This additional quantity is apparently a major factor leading to the aggravating situation of urban flooding in the city of Guwahati. Based on a detailed investigation of the situation in these areas, measures such as the creation of detention/retention ponds/lakes and diversion channels will lead to a reduction in the volume of polluted stormwater running into the city's drainage system. While taking on projects in these areas, the development of holiday resorts with properly designed retention lakes may be an appealing measure. For this type of project, the inter-state cooperation will be necessary. The initiation of a project of this type may be taken up feasibly in a PPP mode.

After all the measures, as briefly discussed above, are adequately and appropriately incorporated in all the drainage basins, the other steps for the improvement of the existing drainage system in the cities/towns facing the issue of urban flooding need to be duly taken in respect of grading, desilting, enhancing the carrying capacity of drains at necessary locations, etc. *(discussed in details under the next subhead).*

1.6. Planning and Designing of Drainage System

Many of the cities/towns facing the issue of urban flooding in our country do not have a properly planned and designed drainage system, despite the fact that there are government policies and guidelines[3,4,5]. The basic requirement for the proper planning of a stormwater drainage system is *the detailed delineation of the watershed/catchment*[3], for which a proper contour map for the urban area concerned must be duly prepared. The catchment area for stormwater does not abide by the political or administrative boundaries of a particular urban area. For instance, the case of Guwahati city may be cited. As shown in figure 1.4, there is a huge catchment area marked as 'A' and 'B' from which an appreciable amount of the storm runoff gets into the city boundary. The consideration of additional catchment areas of this type in the planning and design of the drainage system cannot be ignored.

Based on the catchment area and the contour data, the other parameters, such as rainfall data, flow of storm runoff, including runoff coefficient for long-term planning, have to be duly assessed, as summarised in the government policies and guidelines[3,4,5] for the proper design/redesign of the existing drainage system of an urban area. What is absolutely necessary is the engagement of a competent party for the planning and design of the drainage scheme for an urban area that is in the growing stage of urbanization. A detailed discussion of the various aspects of planning and design of the urban drainage system is beyond the scope of this article. However, the emphasis should be placed on the strict adherence to the guidelines outlined in Volume I of CPHEEO[5] for the engineering design of the urban drainage system. A detailed study of this manual will provide a basic understanding of the planning and design of an urban stormwater drainage system. The integration of rainwater harvesting, recharge systems and detention/retention ponds has become an absolute necessity today. The treatment of storm runoff is also a major consideration for engineering design.

1.7. Operation and Maintenance of Urban Storm Water Drainage System (O&M)

A duly planned, designed, and implemented stormwater drainage system can also, at times, create the problem of urban flooding due to deficient operation and maintenance. In most cities and towns in our country, the lack of proper operations and maintenance (O&M) is a major issue, regardless of the standard of the existing system. The major factors responsible for the lack of proper O&M may be primarily attributed to a lack of adequate knowledge of O&M on the part of ULBs, poor documentation (including inventory) of the drainage system, untrained human resources directly responsible for O&M, an inadequate number of manpower, and inadequate funding, among others. The lack of adequate awareness about their role in matters of O&M of the drainage system is also a concern. As in the case of the proper planning, design, and construction of a stormwater drainage system, adequate technical knowledge, techniques, and tools are available in our country, even for O&M. What is lacking is the proper adoption of the available stock of knowledge, policies, and guidelines.

The salient areas of proper maintenance of the urban drainage system include desilting, removal of solid waste, and removal of sediments from the drains. In fact, each ULB ought to have a well-conceived maintenance manual based on the local conditions and the extent of the area of its town/city. All aspects of O&M of the stormwater drainage system are extensively treated in Volume II of the Manual of the Government of India. All ULBs/UDAs must duly honor the guidelines laid down in this manual.

1.8. Concluding Remarks

The salient aspects of the issue of urban flooding have been briefly dealt with in this article with the objective of drawing the attention of all the stakeholders to the process of urbanization in the country. To address the intensifying urban flooding, technical knowledge, techniques, and tools have been abundantly available for some time, as demonstrated by international studies on this subject so far. Some of the salient works done so far, as well as the standardization of knowledge and guidelines for solving this problem, are reflected in the list of references consulted in writing this chapter. What is strongly felt by the author is the lack of adequate awareness about this stock of standardized knowledge on this problem among the stakeholders, including citizens of cities/towns. Therefore, major efforts need to be directed towards creating this awareness.

What is truly required for each of the towns/cities initially is a master plan for a well-planned and designed drainage system on the basis of the *detailed delineation of the watershed/catchment*[3].

Chapter 2
Different Techniques of Rainwater Harvesting in Urban Areas

2.1. Introduction

As stated by the Under-Secretary of the United Nations[15], *'the biggest challenge with using rainwater harvesting is that it is not included in water policies in many countries. In many cases, water management is based on renewable water sources, which include surface and groundwater, with little consideration given to rainwater.'* This challenge needs to be addressed, since the ***'rainfall and soil water'*** constitute the most important components of the ecosystems (both terrestrial and aquatic). The process of development, coupled with an increase in population taking place, particularly in countries like India, has led to tremendous water pressure both in rural and urban areas. It is in this context that the inclusion of the aspect of rainwater harvesting in the water policies of all countries has been stressed upon by the United Nations[15] for human well-being.

In this chapter, various aspects of rainwater harvesting in urban areas are discussed, as many urban areas in countries like India ***(as briefly addressed in Chapter I of this book)*** face the dual problems of water scarcity and flooding. The rainwater harvesting has been internationally adopted as one of the salient means of mitigating floods and reducing pressures on water resources in urban areas. In view of these two-fold benefits, many countries have been adopting multiple techniques of rainwater harvesting today.

The Government of India has also taken several steps to promote rainwater harvesting and conservation. An account of different steps, as already taken so far in India, has been available in the CPWD Manual[16] of 2019. The salient steps (as mentioned in this Manual) include Master Plan for Artificial Recharge to Ground Water (2013) by Central Ground Water Board (CGWB), the National Water Policy (2012) by Ministry of Water Resources, Advisories issued to States/Union Territories by Central Ground Water Authority (CGWA) for promotion and adoption of artificial recharge to ground water and rainwater harvesting, etc. In addition, there exists the Model Building Bye-Laws, 2016[17], published by the Ministry of Urban Development. The Model Building Bye-Laws has made water harvesting mandatory for all buildings on plots with areas equal to or exceeding 100 sqm. Many ULBs/UDAs in different cities/towns of India have already incorporated the mandatory provision of the Model Building Bye-Laws[17] into their respective bye-laws. However, in most of the cities/towns of the country, this provision does not appear to be strictly enforced on the ground. There are many standards and guidelines[12,13,15,16,17] for the adoption of rainwater harvesting and conservation. A brief discussion about different techniques/methods under different subheads, as summarised in the flowchart of figure 2.1, has been presented herein. The broad subheads chosen for discussion are:

- Storage of rainwater for use and
- Recharging groundwater

The decision to adopt either of the two or both subheads simultaneously depends on the rainfall pattern and its intensity for a particular location. Rainwater broadly consists of two parts: the first part is rainwater falling on the rooftops of different buildings, and the second part is the portion falling directly on the ground surface, which comprises road surfaces, gardens, forests, etc. The second part *(that remains after a small portion is evaporated into the atmosphere and a small portion is absorbed by the top-soil layer)* truly constitutes the rainwater runoff. This runoff forms the stormwater *(as stated in Chapter I)*. Therefore, the harvesting and conservation of rainwater relate to both of these two parts of rainwater. Some of the different techniques/methods are discussed below, with reference to the subheadings described in figure 2.1.

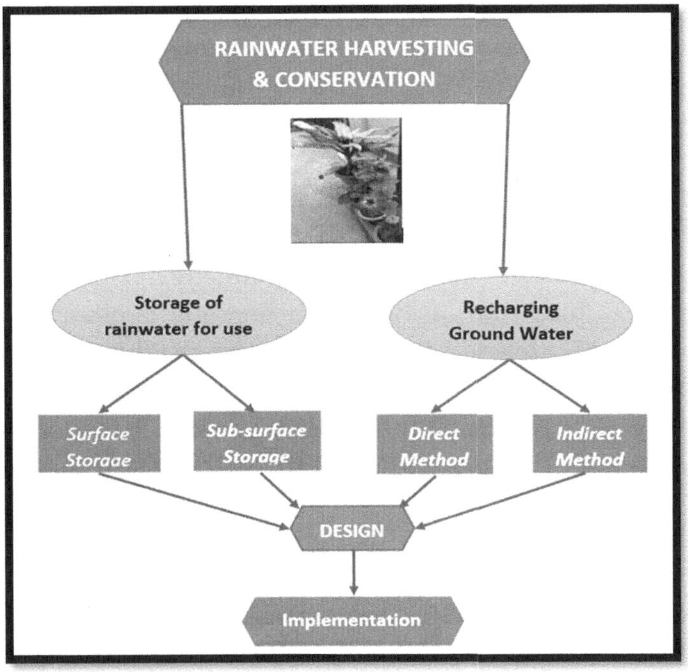

Figure 2.1: Flowchart Showing the Sequence of Subheads for Discussion on Rainwater Harvesting & Conservation (Prepared by the Author)

2.2. Storage of Rainwater for Use (Figure 2.1)

Normally, the storage of rainwater from the rooftops of various types of buildings is taken as recourse to meet the challenges faced by the urban population today. The salient challenges include water scarcity caused by inadequate quantity of water conventionally either from surface sources or from underground sources, and the overflowing of existing urban drainage systems during the monsoon period, thereby causing urban flooding in many cities/towns *(The different aspects of urban flooding have already been dealt with through Chapter I of this book)*. The *storage* of rainwater from the roof and rain runoff (directly falling on the ground) for use has been standardized by the BIS through its guidelines[12,13]. As shown in figure 2.1, the types of storage may be broadly classified as *'Surface storage'* and *'Sub-surface storage'*.

2.2.1. Surface Storage

The first type is adopted for storing rainwater from the rooftop, utilizing a system that is properly planned, designed, and implemented. The system for the storage of rainwater from the roof catchment consists of a number of components. The author *(of this book)* has recently implemented a system for utilizing the rainwater from the roof of a three-story residential building located in the city of Guwahati (Assam). The different components of the "Surface storage' of rainwater from the roof are briefly described below with the help of images shown in image 2.1.

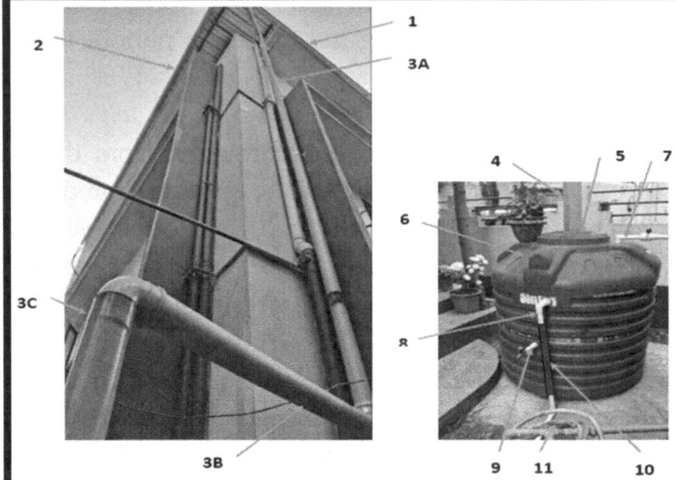

a) Roof, Gutter & Downpipes *b) Surface Storage Tank*

Components: 1. *Pitched Roof (Dyna Roof),* **2**. *Gutter (Cut-HDPE pipe –100mm dia.),* **3A**. *100mm HDPE downpipe (vertical),* **3B**. *100mm HDPE downpipe (horizontal),* **3C**. *100mm HDPE downpipe (vertical) to surface storage tank,* **4**. *100mm downpipe (vertical) in continuity with downpipe 3C,* **5**. *Inlet to Storage Tank,* **6**. *HDPE Storage Tank (Syntex) on ground,* **7**. *PVC pipe connection for pumping rainwater to a second storage tank on ground, 8. PVC pipe connection for recharging ground water through a condemned deep tube well,* **9**. *Water tape for collection of stored rain water through bucket,* **10**. *Online Filter (yet to be installed) and* **11**. *Condemned Deep Tube Well.*

Image 2.1 (b): Images Showing a System of Roof-Top Rainwater Harvesting, Installed in a Three-Storied Residential Building (Photos Taken by the Author)

The main components of this system (numbered as 1 to 11) in the images of image 2.1 (a) and (b) have been noted in the image itself. Apart from the main storage tank marked 6 in the image, there is a provision (marked as 7) of pumping the stored water from this tank to a secondary storage tank during heavy rainfall, thereby increasing the capacity of the storage tanks. In this system, the facility for recharging groundwater simultaneously has also been incorporated, with the help of the component marked 8, through the condemned deep tubewell marked 11 in image 2.1(b). There has been provision for incorporating an online filter marked 10 in the image. This filter will be installed at the position marked 10 or in a suitable position on the downpipe marked 3C, once the detailed specifications are obtained from the manufacturer. The level of the inlet for recharging groundwater (component 8 in the figure) through the condemned tubewell has been so chosen as to facilitate the use of a sufficient quantity of stored water for different purposes, such as watering kitchen gardens and plants, car washing, etc. A tape at the lowest level of the tank has been provided on the back side *(opposite to the side having components 9 & 10)* for the purpose of cleaning. The major considerations to be made while planning, designing and implementing a system of this type will be briefly discussed later under the subhead *'Design'*.

The tank shown in image 2.1(b) is an HDPE one. However, depending on the design requirements and capacity, other types of tanks, such as those made of brickwork, Ferrocement, or RCC, may be used.

The system of gutters and downpipes adopted for a pitched roof, as shown in image 2.1, will obviously be different for a flat roof. For a reinforced concrete flat roof, the proper treatment of the rooftop will be provided to the outlets with a suitable slope. Thereafter, the arrangement of downpipes to the surface tank (as shown in figure 2.1) will have to be adopted. The author (of this book) successfully adopted a drain system, as briefly described in figure 2.2, for the collection of rainwater from the flat roof of a four-story hospital building designed and executed by him at Jorhat (Assam).

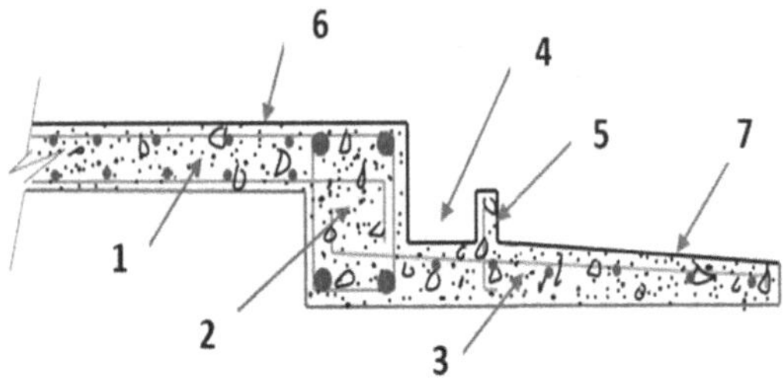

Components: ***1.*** *R.C.C. slab,* ***2.*** *R.C.C. Edge beam,* ***3.*** *R.C.C. Chaja,* ***4.*** *R.C.C. Drain for collection of roof-rainwater,* ***5.*** *R.C.C. side wall of drain,* ***6.*** *Concrete topping with neat finish on roof slab with proper slope to drain (marked 4) and* ***7.*** *Neat cement finish (over plaster) on top and sides of chaja & drain. (Reinforcements only symbolically shown for the R.C.C. components).*

Figure 2.2: Schematic Diagram Showing the Arrangements of Drain for Collection of Roof-Rainwater from Flat Roof

The downpipes may be provided at suitable locations along the drain, as shown in figure 2.2, and connected to the surface storage tank *(as shown in image 2.1)*. For a system of this type, the treatment of the rooftop is an important aspect. This treatment must provide the proper gradient to facilitate the flow of rainwater from the rooftop to the side drains on the sides of the edge beams, as shown in figure 2.2. The topping provided for this building was the cement concrete of an appropriate grade. Alternative arrangements *(in lieu of the arrangement shown in figure 2.2)* may also be made for collecting rainwater from a flat roof by providing a system of downpipes to surface storage tanks, incorporating inlets *(for the downpipes)* at suitable locations.

2.2.2. Sub-surface Storage

The situation of a sub-surface *(underground)* storage arises in cases where a plot has a large roof area and a substantially large uncovered area, yielding an appreciable quantity of rainwater runoff. Depending on the catchment area, there are different traditional techniques of storing rainwater on the surface. These techniques[16] include *'underground tanks, ponds, check dams, weirs, etc.'* For plots of moderate size, such as domestic or industrial plots, underground tanks of masonry or reinforced concrete have been commonly used elsewhere. The sizes of this type of tank are dependent on design considerations *(to be briefly dealt with at a later stage under the subhead of Design, as indicated in figure 2.1).*

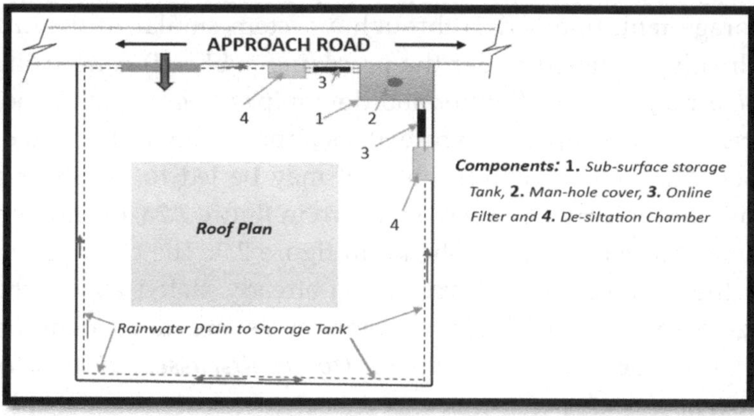

Figure 2.3: Layout Plan Showing the Salient Components for the Use of Sub-Surface Rainwater Storage Tank (Prepared by the Author)

Figure 2.3 illustrates a general layout for the various components required to install a sub-surface storage tank (marked 1) on a plot with a sufficiently large roof area and numerous open areas for gardening and parking purposes. The storage will be designed as an RCC one with an RCC cover slab having a manhole (marked 2) for purposes of cleaning. Since it is a large plot, the rainwater drains will be laid along the sides, as indicated in the figure, with the gradient provided as indicated by the arrows. The desiltation chamber (marked 4 in the figure) is an important component for arresting silts and other debris carried by rainwater runoff.

A screen of suitable material needs to be appropriately placed at the outlet of this chamber to arrest floating debris, such as paper and leaves. The top of the desiltation chamber is commonly kept open. The online filter (marked 3 in the figure) becomes necessary for removing pollutants that are carried by the runoff. The common practice has been to allow the domestic wastewater into the side drains. This is particularly apparent in urban areas that lack a separate sewer system.

The rainwater from the rooftop will also be led to the storage tank (marked 1) through a system similar to the one (already discussed under the preceding subhead) comprising the arrangements of gutter and downpipes (Figure 2a) or roof drain and downpipes (Figure 3), as appropriate to the type of roof. The rainwater from the roof may be led to the storage tank through HDPE pipes, as shown in figure 2.2a, or through the rainwater drains, as shown in figure 2.3. The choice is up to the designer of the system. As already stated above, the sizes/capacities of different components are dependent on different design considerations ***(to be discussed at a later stage).***

2.3. Recharging Ground Water (as per Flowchart of Figure 2.1)

In many areas *(both rural and urban),* the depletion of groundwater has been a common phenomenon, basically on account of its withdrawal for different types of use at a rate much higher than that of its replenishment under natural conditions. The major portion of rainwater runoff returns to rivers or oceans through stormwater drainage systems in urban areas. It is in this context that rainwater harvesting for recharging groundwater through artificial structures has assumed immense importance in both urban and rural areas. As stated in Chapter I of this book, stresses to an appreciable extent are being laid on rainwater harvesting by the Government of India[2,3,4,5,6]. A discussion on different types of artificial structures for recharging groundwater in urban areas has been briefly attempted herein under two broad subheads: **Direct Method** and **Indirect Method** *(as already indicated in figure 2.1).*

2.3.1. Direct Method (As Per Flowchart of Figure 2.1)

There are broadly two types[2,6,7] of direct methods of artificial recharge: (a) Surface Spreading Techniques and (b) Sub-Surface Techniques, as briefly described below.

2.3.1.1. Surface Spreading Techniques:

- *Flooding:* The surface runoff is spread over a larger area by making suitable arrangements (such as side embankments) so that it remains over the area for a sufficiently long time to facilitate the recharge of the groundwater body. The area for spreading the runoff must have a favourable hydro-geological situation.
- *Basins or Percolation Tanks:* These are artificially created conservation structures for recharging groundwater by storing rainwater. These structures are typically adopted in both rural and urban areas. This type of rainwater conservation appears to be very useful in the low-lying foothills located on the south-eastern side of Guwahati City (Assam), through which rainwater enters the city from a large catchment on the adjoining hills.
- *Ditch and Furrows:* It is an effective technique adopted for enhancing soil moisture mostly in dryland farming, horticulture and reforestation. The technique consists of digging parallel ditches (trenches) and furrows (shallow channels) along the natural slope of the land. The runoff collected in the ditch percolates into the soil slowly, thereby improving the soil moisture.

- *Stream Augmentation:* This technique is a very useful one for recharging groundwater. The essence of this technique consists of artificially increasing the area of seepage of a natural river or stream by arresting the runoff by constructing a series of check dams and/or widening the river/stream beds at suitable locations.
- *Surface Irrigation:* The surface irrigation adopted to increase crop production from additional water sources also contributes to recharging groundwater.

2.3.1.2. Sub-surface Techniques

These techniques are adopted to take surface runoff into the deeper aquifer, particularly in areas where the top layers are impermeable. Some of these techniques[2,6,7] are briefly described below.

- *Recharge Well (or Injection Well):* A description of a recharge well for a building plot is given in figure 2.4. The salient components ***(marked as 1 to 12)*** necessary for implementing this scheme are noted in the figure itself.

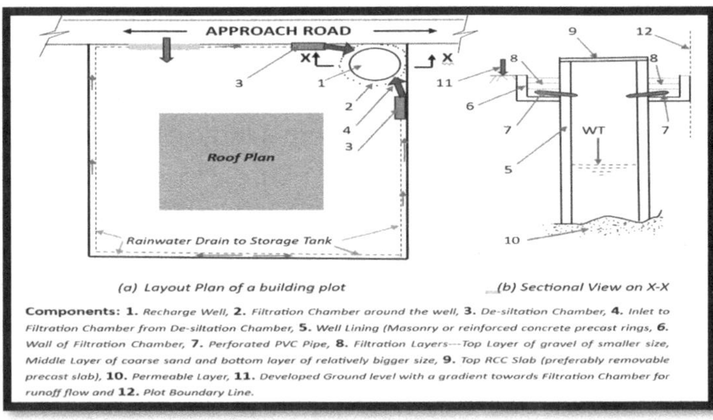

Figure 2.4: Layout Plan Showing the Position and the Sectional View of a Recharge Well For a Building Plot Indicating Different Components (Prepared by the Author)

The physical dimensions and structural details of various components, such as the well, filtration chamber, and drains, are dependent on design considerations *(to be addressed at a later stage)*. The recharge well can be utilized for both recharge and pumping out stored water for use. In addition, an abandoned dug well or bore well can also be suitably utilized as a recharge well. On the other hand, the recharge well can also be used to inject water from other available sources, as needed.

- *Recharge Trench:* The recharge trenches are normally adopted in places where permeable layers are available at a shallow depth. This type of structure is preferred for building plots, beds of ephemeral rivers or streams *(ephemeral rivers or streams are those that have water flow only during the monsoon period, remaining dry for most of the rest of the year)*. An arrangement of recharge trench has been described below in figure 2.5.

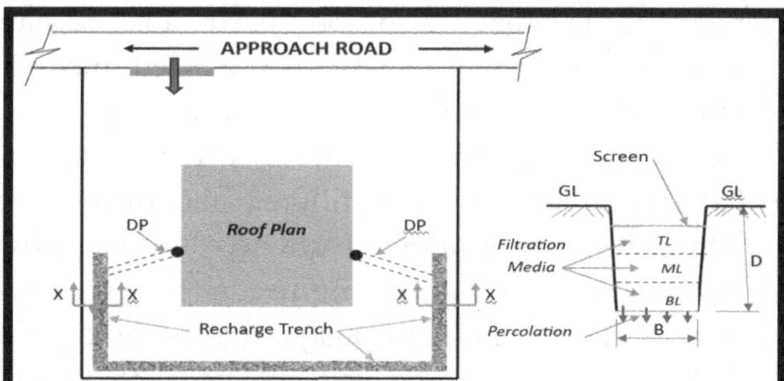

a) Layout plan of a building plot showing Recharge Trench *b) Sectional View on X-X*

***Symbols used in the figure**: **DP**---Down Pipe system for roof-top rainwater, **GL**---Developed Ground Level, **D**--- Depth to bottom of Trench, **B**----Breadth of the trench at the bottom, **TL**—Top Layer of filtration media, **ML**---Middle Layer of filtration media and **BL**---Bottom Layer of filtration media.*

Figure 2.5: Plan of the Plot with Roof Plan and Layout of Recharge Trench & Sectional View of the Trench
(Prepared By Author)

The depth (D), breadth (B) and length of the recharge trench are dependent on the design considerations *(dealt with under the subhead of Design).* However, as recommended by CPWD Guidelines[16], the depth and breadth normally range between (1.0 to 1.5 m) and (0.5 to 1.0 m) respectively. The sides are given a mild slope for stability. The filtration media normally contains three layers marked as TL, ML and BL in figure 2.5 (b). The bottom layer consists of boulders and gravel of relatively larger size; the middle layer is composed of boulders and gravel finer than those in the bottom layer, and the top layer is made up of Coarse sand or very fine gravel. The developed GL is given a mild slope towards the trench to facilitate the flow of runoff into the trench. A screen of wire mesh may be placed either on top of the filtration media (as shown in the figure) or on top of the trench to arrest leaves or other types of debris. The rainwater drains (if any) may also be connected to the trench as appropriate. The downpipe system (provided for the collection of rainwater from the roof) may also be suitably linked with the trench.

- *Gravity-Head Recharge Well:* Normal dug wells and bore wells may also be used for recharging groundwater. This technique is preferred in situations where the plot area is limited and a deep aquifer is overlaid by impermeable strata. The rainwater to be led into wells has to be filtered and disinfected. In addition, the condition of gravity-flow of rainwater into the well through piping needs to be created at a certain head. Simultaneously, the pumping of the water from the recharge wells for use is also possible.
- *Recharge Pit:* The recharge pits are considered useful for shallow aquifers and small plots with small buildings. As recommended by NWM Guidelines[6], the pits have a width in the range of 1 to 2m and a depth in the range of 2 to 3m. The pit needs to be filled with pebbles and boulders. On the other hand, rainwater

from rainwater drains and roof downpipes should be led to the recharge pits through a desiltation chamber or a filtration chamber to arrest debris and ensure disinfection *(as discussed earlier).*

- *Recharge Shaft:* Similar to the recharge pit, the recharge shaft is also adopted when the aquifer to be recharged is located at a shallow depth. The diameter to be drilled manually or by a drilling machine ranges from 1 to 3m, while the depth ranges from 2 to 12m, as recommended by the guidelines. The shaft so created needs to be filled with filtration media[6] comprising boulders, coarse gravel and fine gravel.

There are other types of sub-surface techniques such as Connector well[7], Natural openings & Cavity fillings[2], Bore hole flooding[2], etc. A discussion on these techniques has been deliberately avoided, since the techniques briefly discussed herein *(as dealt with in the preceding paragraphs)* are the ones *(under direct methods)* commonly adopted for recharging groundwater in the building plots of urban areas.

2.3.2. Indirect Method (as per Flowchart of Figure 2.1)

There are broadly two types of indirect methods, as given in the NWM Guidelines6: (a) Induced Recharge from surface water source and (b) Aquifer Modification. However, other literatures[2,7] include various other sub-types as well. All these techniques are outside the scope of this discussion, as the focus herein is on the techniques commonly adopted for recharging groundwater with rainwater in urban areas.

2.4. Design (As Per Flowchart of Figure 2.1)

The design aspects of rainwater harvesting have been discussed in different guidelines[2,6,8]. The salient aspects of designing a particular rainwater-harvesting system have been presented herein with reference to the subheads summarized in the Flowchart of figure 2.6.

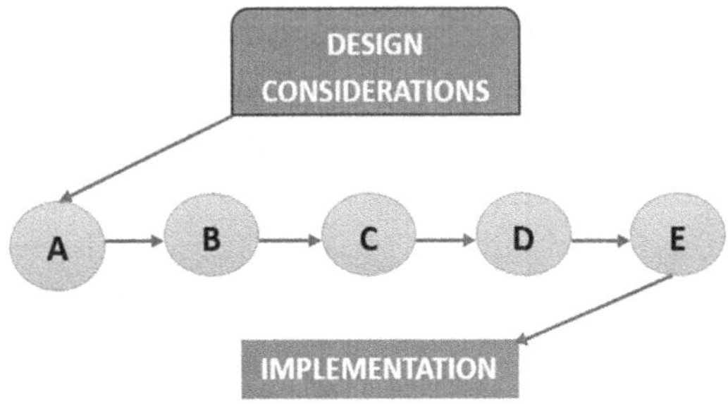

Subheads: **A.** *Assessment of the catchment area and rainfall pattern,* **B.** *Decision about the intended use of the harvested rainwater,* **C.** *Selection of the suitable system of harvesting,* **D.** *Design of the chosen system and* **E.** *Detailing and working out the total cost of the designed system.*

Figure 2.6: Flowchart Showing Different Considerations for Design of a System of Rainwater Harvesting (Prepared By Author)

2.4.1 Assessment of the Catchment Area and Rainfall Pattern (A in Figure 2.6)

The designer of a rainwater-harvesting system needs to initially assess the total quantity of rainwater available for harvesting. For this purpose, the necessary rainfall data, including intensity, frequency, and duration, for a specific location (district and state) are required. These data may be obtained from meteorological observations made by the country's Meteorological Department. In addition, the catchment area providing the runoff (both from rooftop and ground surface) for the plot *(may it be residential/industrial/commercial/educational/or any other type)* has to be duly assessed. Based on these data, the quantity of available rainwater for harvesting has to be calculated, as broadly explained by the guidelines[2,6].

2.4.2. Decision about the Intended Use of the Harvested Rainwater (B in Figure 2.6)

To select a suitable system, the primary purpose of harvesting rainwater must be determined. Its intended use may include one or more purposes, such as irrigation, washing toilets, providing drinking water, and recharging the groundwater aquifer, among others. Based on the chosen purpose of harvesting, the quality of harvested water required needs to be ascertained based on the available standards. It is only the required quality that will determine the type of filtration unit to be adopted in a particular rainwater harvesting system. The filtration aspect assumes greater importance in the case of the runoff that carries chemicals harmful to the intended purpose.

2.4.3. Selection of the Suitable System of Harvesting (C in Figure 2.6)

The selection of a suitable system must be based on the type of harvesting, i.e., whether the system is required for rooftop rainwater alone, for surface runoff only, or for both. Thereafter, the different components *(such as those dealt with under the subheads of 'Storage of Rainwater for use'* and *'Recharging ground water')* will need to be determined, depending on the intended purpose of harvesting, the available quantity, and the required quality of the harvested water.

2.4.4. Design of the Chosen System (D in Figure 2.6)

The components of the system, as selected, will be designed and finalized in respect of sizes/capacities, specifications, etc, with due regard to different guidelines[2,6,8] and standards[4,5]. In the case of the design of recharge structures, a correct identification of the aquifers to be recharged becomes an absolute necessity. This is facilitated by the strata chart of a bore hole drilled in or around the location of the project of rainwater harvesting.

2.4.5. Detailing and Working Out the Total Cost of the Designed System (E in Figure 2.6)

The detailed drawings of all components, along with the specifications for each unit of the designed system, will be prepared to calculate the total cost and facilitate implementation. The total cost of the project is crucial for the owner's consideration of the benefits that will accrue from its implementation. The diverse benefits of rainwater harvesting and conservation are briefly noted in the concluding remark of this article.

2.5. Implementation of the System

Once a rainwater harvesting system has been duly planned and designed, as briefly discussed under the subheads shown in figure 2.6, its implementation at the site must be carried out by a team well-experienced in the execution of similar projects, under the technical person involved in the design stage of the system. The different components of the system will be installed as per the layout plan and detailed drawings. The experiences of the author in the execution of projects of rainwater harvesting suggest a lump-sum contract (as labour cost—all items of the system being procured by the Owner) to be awarded to the team implementing the project on the ground.

2.6. Maintenance and Operation of the System

Any system designed for rainwater harvesting requires proper maintenance and operation to ensure durable service and efficiency in delivering the intended benefits. Different aspects of maintenance and operation are briefly discussed with reference to the subheads summarized in figure 2.7.

2.6.1. Maintenance

- *Catchment Area (both rooftop & ground surface) — **A** in figure 2.7:* These areas need to be cleaned at regular intervals so that the runoff remains free from leaves and other types of debris. The screens (if provided in the system) should also be kept clean. The use of any paint or chemical on the catchment surface has to be totally avoided. In addition, special care has to be taken to thoroughly clean the entire catchment surface, including the gutters and downpipe system (if provided in the system), prior to the onset of every monsoon season.
- *Diversion of the First Flush over Catchment Area (**B** in figure 2.7):* The first flush (by rainfall) of the monsoon season needs to be diverted from entry into the storage tank or recharging structure, particularly in case the harvesting system does not have components like the filtration unit. This measure is necessary for avoiding dirt and chemicals. For this type of diversion, a suitable mechanism through the provision of the valve and pipes will have to be incorporated into the system of rainwater harvesting.

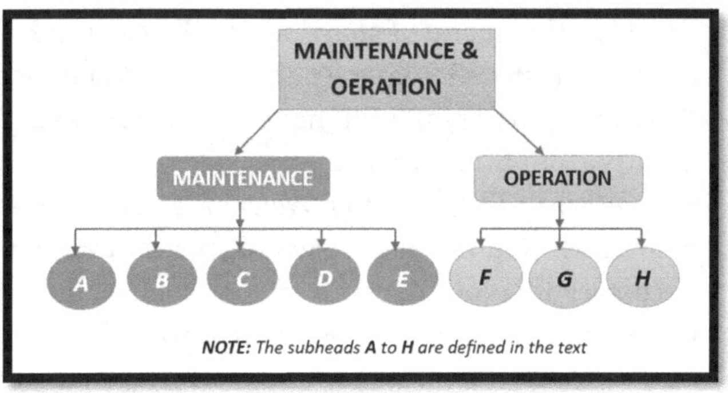

Figure 2.7: Summary of Subheads Chosen for Maintenance & Operation

- *Filtration and Desiltation/Settlement Units (**C** in figure 2.7):* The cleaning of the filtration/desiltation chambers of the rainwater harvesting systems has to be done periodically for proper functioning. Special attention needs to be paid to aspects such as the replacement of filtration media (as required), removal of sludge built up in desiltation/settlement tanks, and checking of UV filters (if used), among others.
- *Storage Tanks (**D** in figure 2.7):* The contamination, breeding of mosquitoes, cracks, leaks, etc., are common problems in storage tanks adopted for various types of rainwater in the harvesting systems. Periodic inspection to be followed by corrective measures, as necessary, will have to be taken.
- *Recharge Structures (**E** in figure 2.7):* The recharge structures, when used for recharging the groundwater, will also be maintained well. The desilting of percolation pits/trenches/wells (if adopted in the system) has to be done periodically. Similarly, for other recharge structures such as dug wells/ bore wells, the inlets and outlets need to be checked periodically so that they do not get clogged.

2.6.2. Operation

- *Checking the quality of stored water (**F** in figure 2.7):* The quality of stored water (particularly when used for drinking purposes) will have to be checked for its quality from time to time.
- *Prevention of Stagnation of Water in Storage Tank (**G** in figure 2.7):* Regular use of water in the storage tank is necessary to avoid harmful effects, such as the creation of bad odours, breeding of insects/mosquitoes, etc. The outlet from the storage tank, which facilitates the overflow water to flow directly into the nearest stormwater drain, must be kept clean.

- *Seasonal Measures (**H** in figure 2.7):* At the end of each monsoon season, all components of the system will have to be duly checked to identify the defects, if any. The defects, if found, need to be corrected. In addition, all the remaining dirt and sediments may be cleared off necessarily by flushing the affected components with clean water.

2.7. Concluding Remarks

The primary objective of this chapter is to raise public awareness, particularly among urban area residents, who face the dual challenges of water scarcity and urban flooding. How the rainwater harvesting and conservation contribute towards the solution of these problems substantially has been stressed upon in this chapter, rather than the extensive treatment of the design aspects as dealt with in different guidelines and standards *(as given under references)* of different systems for harvesting and conservation of rainwater.

The benefits of rainwater harvesting and conservation in urban areas are manifold. The salient benefits include mitigation of urban flooding, augmentation of water supply to citizens, reduction of soil erosion in hilly zones, and economic benefits to citizens who adopt individual systems for their own plots, such as savings on water and energy bills, as well as a contribution towards sustainable water management.

The ULBs/UDAs are expected to initiate appropriate schemes on their own in public areas, apart from creating some schemes to provide incentives in suitable forms to individual citizens adopting individual measures of rainwater harvesting and conservation.

Chapter 3

Public Awareness: A Salient Aspect of the Management of Urban Drainage System

3.1. Introduction

Urban flooding has become a major problem, raising serious concerns internationally during the urbanization process. In India, too, this problem has been intensifying. The factors appearing in the flowchart of figure 3.1 have already been briefly dealt with in the last two chapters of this book.

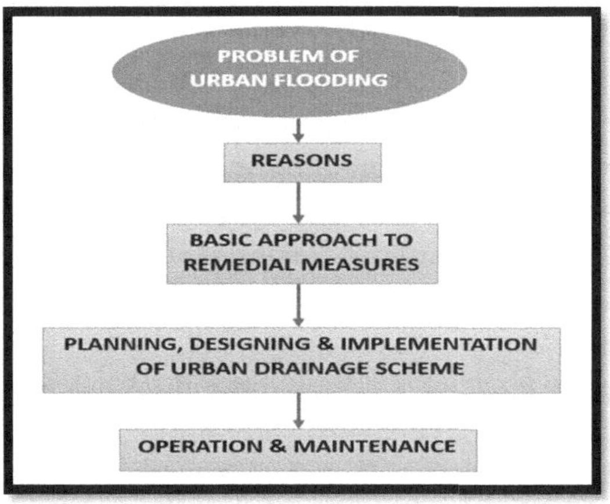

Figure 3.1: Flowchart Showing the Factors Already Dealt with in Relation to Urban Flooding

Once a properly planned, designed and implemented Urban Drainage System (UDS) has been in place for any city/town, the proper management of the same becomes an absolute necessity to ensure that it (UDS) continues to serve the objectives, as conceived in planning and design for its intended period of life. There have been many cases of urban flooding even in cities/towns having properly planned, designed and implemented UDS. This type of situation is primarily caused by various lapses in its proper management. Therefore, the adoption of all measures necessary for the appropriate management of the UDS in line with the available policies, guidelines and technology, as evidenced by different publications *(some of which appear under the list of references given below),* has been absolutely necessary for getting rid of the likely damages caused by urban flooding.

The Ministry of Housing and Urban Affairs, Government of India, published Manual[5] on Storm Water Drainage System (SWDS) in two volumes. Part C of Volume II of this Manual deals with different aspects of the management of UDS. Most of the cities/towns in India do not appear to have honored the guidelines well-set in this Manual. The gamut of an efficient management of UDS encompasses primarily four broad aspects5. These are: *Public Awareness, Institutional Arrangement, Capacity Building and Training* and *Financial Management and Sustainable Operation and Maintenance.* The scope of this chapter has been limited to creating public awareness, given its pivotal role in the efficient functioning of the UDS.

3.2. Creation of Public Awareness

The issue of urban flooding in many Indian cities and towns has been intensifying due to several reasons, as briefly discussed in the last two chapters of the book. The lack of public awareness about the roles to be played by urban citizens in the management of the UDS has been well-recognized as a major aspect warranting the attention of all stakeholders in urban areas. The lack of public awareness is abundantly clear from the observed uses of stormwater drains by the public for purposes such as:

- Receptacles for dumping garbage, wastes from demolition and construction activities,

- Encroachment on the sides of drains for different purposes,
- Allowing sewage water to flow directly into drains, etc.

The chronic problems of these types have been responsible for a substantial increase in the costs of operation and maintenance of UDS, apart from reducing its designed utility period.

Therefore, creating public awareness has become an internationally recognized strategy for managing UDS. In India too, the Manual[5] of MoHUA *(Vol II: Part C)* deals with different aspects relating to the creation of public awareness, based on the basic mechanism of Information, Education and Communication (IEC). A brief discussion on the creation of public awareness has been attempted herein in pursuit of the subheads summarized through the flowchart appearing in figure 3.2.

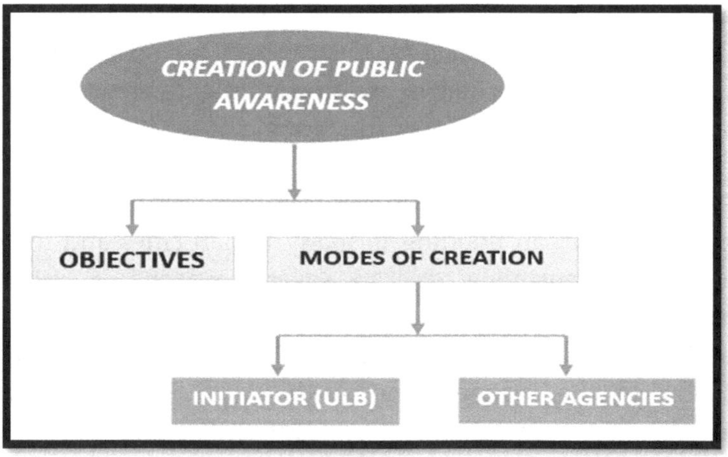

Figure 3.2: Flowchart Depicting the Subheads for Discussion

3.2.1. Major Objectives

The major objectives to be achieved by creating public awareness are indicated in figure 3.3.

- *Rainwater Harvesting:* The citizens of the urban area have to develop the culture of harvesting rainwater in their respective plots for the reasons dealt with earlier *(last two chapters).* The different methods of harvesting do exist in standardized forms [11,12,13]. What is needed now is to create awareness among the citizens for the adoption of different feasible measures *(as already discussed under Chapter II).*
- *No Sewage in SWDs:* It has been commonly observed in many locations of the urban areas that the sewage (mostly from septic tanks having no soak-pits) is allowed to fall into Storm Water Drains. This type of practice is clearly indicative of the lack of awareness about its adverse impacts on the surrounding environment.
- *No Dumping in SWDs:* Many urban citizens still have the habit of littering and dumping debris and different wastes in the stormwater drains. At times, people are seen to go for open defecation into the drains. Therefore, the awareness about the adverse impacts on the functioning and life of stormwater drains needs to be created among the citizens. Even in cases of covered drains, such as footpaths, the top slabs at some locations are found to be broken or displaced, creating gaps for the dumping of debris.

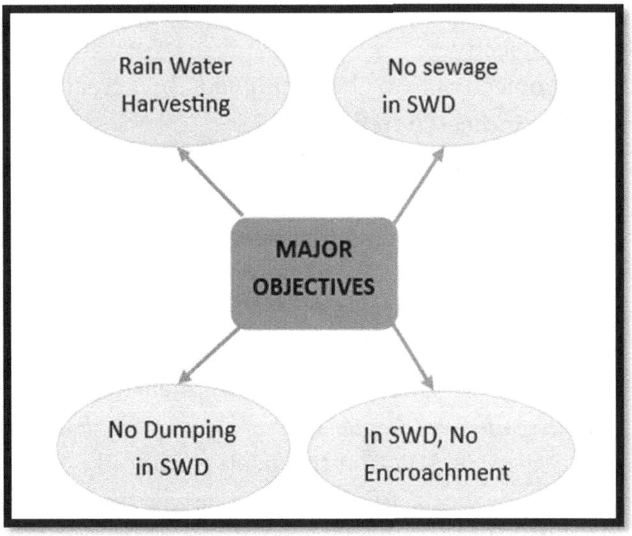

Figure 3.3: Major Objectives of Creating Public Awareness (Based on the Guidelines[5] of MoHUA)

No Encroachments in SWDs: The encroachment on the sides of stormwater drains (particularly on the banks of natural drains passing through urban areas) for various purposes has been a chronic problem. The creation of public awareness about the harmful impact of this culture becomes an absolute necessity.

3.2.2. Modes of Creation of Public Awareness (Figure 3.2)

Broadly, there are two parties involved in the process of creating public awareness about the proper operation and management of urban SWDs, as indicated in figure 3.2. A brief discussion of each of these two parties is presented below.

- *Initiator:* The primary responsibility of creating public awareness obviously rests with the department of Town & Country Planning of the States/UTs, since the ULBs/UDAs come under its jurisdiction. The concerned ULB/UDA needs to design a public awareness campaign to educate citizens about the importance of the IEC strategy, as outlined in various guidelines[5,15]. The public awareness aims to bring about a **behavioural change** relating to salient points stated under the sub-head *'Objective'* above among the urban citizens. Other aspects of public education include: **Community Involvement, Policy Support and Resilience Building.**

Different leaflets and pamphlets may be prepared for public awareness and education of citizens in the language appropriate to the target audience in respective urban areas. The contents of the leaflets, pamphlets, and other materials prepared may be communicated to urban citizens through various modes of communication, as briefly discussed below.

- *Modes of Communication:* The possible modes of communication to the public are well outlined in Manual[5] of MoHUA *(Part C—Vol II)*. The salient ones include print media, social media, electronic media, mobile phones, educational institutions, and voluntary organizations, among others. In educational institutions, events such as seminars, workshops, model competitions, and debates can be organized on topics related to raising awareness among the public about their roles in the sustainable management of urban stormwater drainage systems. Even projects in undergraduate and postgraduate courses may be assigned to students on various aspects of creating public awareness. For example, the appropriate topics for projects may relate to the necessity of rainwater harvesting (including different methods). The leaflets, pamphlets, and hoardings may be displayed in cinema halls, public transports, etc.

The ULBs/UDAs have different wards in place in their respective cities/towns. The Ward Commissioner may take the initiative in forming local committees or groups with local enthusiasts (such as students or other residents) to popularize the various measures formulated for creating public awareness about the sustainable management of drainage systems. There should be a feasible mechanism for constructive discussion between the concerned ULB/UAD and local committees to achieve the objectives of public awareness *(as briefly discussed above).*

3.3. *Concluding Remarks*

The initiators, as already stated herein, are the ULBs/UDAs responsible for the initiation and implementation of the various measures, briefly discussed in this chapter. Obviously, the extent of success in implementing measures to create public awareness about sustainable management among urban citizens is dependent on the institutional arrangements, capabilities in terms of knowledge, skills, and finance, as well as the ethical values of the members of the concerned government and ULB/UDA.

The participation of the local citizens is equally important. Therefore, the local committees of citizens *(as stated above)* also have a significant role to play in ensuring the proper functioning of the urban SWDs. There are some committees of citizens contributing appreciably towards this end in some of the cities/towns of India.

References

1. United Nations. (n.d.). *Guidelines for reducing flood losses*. Retrieved from
    a. https://www.un.org/esa/sustdev/publications
2. Singh, D. (n.d.). *Compendium report 22*. International Centre for Environmental Audit and Sustainable Development (iCED). Retrieved from https://iced.cag.gov.in/uploads/Series2
3. National Disaster Management Authority (NDMA). (2010). *National disaster management guidelines: Management of urban flooding* (ISBN: 978-93-80440-09-5). Government of India.
4. India Water Partnership. (2020, December). *Urban flood management: Drainage and planning*. Retrieved from https://www.cwp-india.org
5. Central Public Health and Environmental Engineering Organization (CPEEO), Ministry of Housing and Urban Affairs. (2019, May). *Manual on storm water drainage system* (Vol. 1: Part A: Engineering design; Vol. 2: Part B: Operation and maintenance; Part C: Management). Retrieved from https://mohua.gov.in
6. Weather Underground. (n.d.). *Guwahati, India weather history*. Retrieved from https://wunderground.com/history/monthly/in/Guwahati
7. India Today. (2024, August 1). Retrieved from https://www.indiatoday.in/India

8. Rainwater Harvesting. (n.d.). *Average rainfall of states in India*. Retrieved from https://www.rainwaterharvesting.org
9. Connective Cities. (n.d.). *Guwahati city profile in terms of drainage system and GMDA's initiative in nature-based solutions*. Retrieved from https://community.connective-cities.net
10. Guwahati Metropolitan Development Authority (GMDA). (n.d.). *Mission flood free Guwahati*. Retrieved from https://assam.gov.in
11. Central Public Works Department (CPWD). (2019). *Rainwater harvesting & conservation manual*. New Delhi: Author.
12. Bureau of Indian Standards. (2008). *IS 15797: Roof top rainwater harvesting—Guidelines*.
13. Bureau of Indian Standards. (2001). *IS 14961: Guidelines for rainwater harvesting in hilly areas by roof water collection system*.
14. Government of Assam, Department of Housing and Urban Affairs. (2022, October 15). *Assam unified building construction (regulation) byelaws, 2022* (The Assam Gazette Notification).
15. Stormwater2030. (n.d.). *Public awareness and education in storm water management*. Retrieved from https://stormwater2030.org